To the greatest guy Anton on Earth

Be[...]
Christine

HOW TO INTERPRET YOUR DREAMS USING A PENDULUM

CHRISTINE VANDERNOOT

Cognitrix Ltd.
London, U.K.

© Christine VanderNoot, 2009

Christine VanderNoot has asserted her right under the Copyright, Designs and Patents Act, 1988, to be identified as author of this work.
Illustrations by Christine VanderNoot

All rights reserved.
No part of this book may be reproduced, utilised or stored in any form or by any means, electronic or mechanical, without prior permission from the author.

Except for the personal examples from myself and my husband all other examples are fictitious and are meant only to illustrate particular ideas in the book.

> Neither dowsing nor the interpretation of your dreams are an excuse to harm yourself or others. Interpreting your dreams does not excuse you from moral, ethical and legal behaviour!

Published by Cognitrix Ltd, London, U.K.
ISBN: 978-0-9562487-0-1

Printed and bound in Great Britain by
CPI Antony Rowe, Chippenham and Eastbourne

British Library Cataloguing in Publication data available

A French version of this book is available under the title "*Comment Interpréter Vos Rêves Avec Un Pendule*".

For Romain, my nephew and godson

Contents

Acknowledgements   *ix*

Glossary   *xi*

Introduction   1

Three Important Points Before Going Further   7

So What Are Dreams Anyway?   13

How to Interpret Your Dreams   21

Some More Examples of Dream Interpretation   53

Tips for Dream Interpretation   69

Basics of Using A Pendulum   75

Acknowledgements

This book wouldn't exist without the help and encouragement of the following people. My appreciation and thanks go to:

My husband **Ted** for ideas, discussions and patience.

Robin Winbow who taught me how to dowse and encouraged me to explore further.

My friends **Christian-Rudolph Krämer, Jacqueline Power, Katriona Shawki, Layo Nathan,** and **Tina Duffy** for reading early drafts and giving me their comments and support.

Glossary

Aspects of the person: physical, mental, emotional, energetic aspects.

Whole being: physically AND emotionally AND mentally AND energetically.

Parts of the person: feminine side, masculine side, ego*.

Ego*: self-image which is the sum of our beliefs, values and behaviours learned from others or from experience (conditioning).

Conscious: those thoughts and feelings of which we are explicitly aware.

Unconscious: those thoughts and feelings of which we are not normally aware. This can often be experienced as a vague feeling or felt sense.

Natural self: instinctive responses we are born with or who we are, naturally, before conditioning is acquired.

Symbolism: representation of one thing by another. This representation comes from *our personal associations* of words, objects, people, feelings, numbers, colours, sounds, smells, etc, resulting from *our* life experiences.

The above glossary is intended to give you an idea of what I have in mind when I use a particular term in this book. I am not trying to convince anyone of *my* beliefs. My intention is only to communicate my approach to interpreting dreams.

Introduction

This way to discover a simple Do-It-Yourself approach to interpreting your dreams using the pendulum. It is based upon:

what questions to ask and the order in which to ask them.

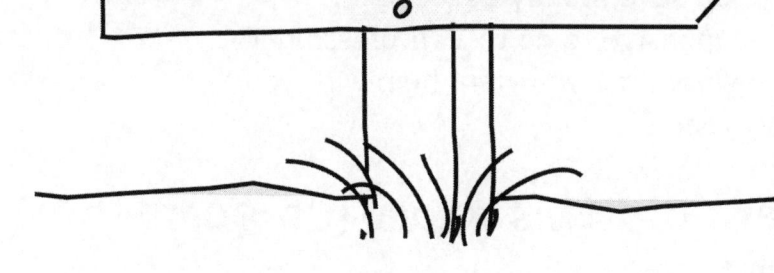

If you don't know how to use a pendulum, then begin with "Basics of Using A Pendulum", page 75.

Benefits of this approach

- 👍 Your dreams remain private unless you want to tell someone;
- 👍 You find your own symbolism;
- 👍 Nobody else forces their interpretation on your dreams;
- 👍 Your intuition and creativity guide you;
- 👍 You interpret your dreams when it is convenient for you;
- 👍 You go at your own pace;
- 👍 You can return to a dream as many times as you want;
- 👍 You save money because it is expensive to go to a "professional" every time you want help with your dreams.

Where did this approach come from?

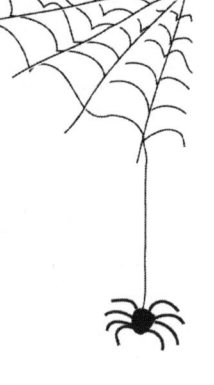

It all began ten years ago when I became interested in my dreams. My interest arose because I kept having dreams with spiders. The number of spiders was increasing until they were absolutely everywhere, even a big tarantula covering my whole face! It was time I found out what was going on. First I looked in a lot of books on dreams but I was confused because the books said spiders represented: mother as an object of fear; feminine devouring affection; aggression; progressive development; luck, etc. What was that all about? Where did these definitions come from? Which one was right for me and how could I know? Of course, the definition "luck" was tempting but was it really what *my* spiders represented? Even after reading these definitions I continued to dream of spiders, so I knew the books hadn't helped me to understand what spiders meant. I realised I had to look somewhere else. I went to a "professional" who made me draw a spider. I drew a big friendly spider with a lot of baby spiders on it and again I felt stuck at that point. I kept looking at my drawing, thinking "What does it mean?" This is when my pendulum came to mind. At that time I was already using it to answer questions about which foods or vitamins were good for me, so I decided to use the pendulum to find out what the drawing meant. I was surprised to discover that, for me, spiders symbolised children. That was very unexpected and I became curious.

What was it about spiders that reminded me of children? Why had my unconscious mind picked this image to represent children? First, I asked questions about spiders and I realised that I was uneasy with spiders because they were unpredictable. I never knew when and where they would run next. Then I remembered that I was never at ease around children and I never knew why until I understood this dream. My uneasiness with children was because, for me, children were also unpredictable. When I was with children I was never sure if they were going to laugh or cry or run into the street, and I realised I was not comfortable with this unpredictability. I was amazed by this discovery. Once I understood this I stopped dreaming of spiders! Even more amazing was that the next time I was with children I was completely relaxed around them. I finally understood why I had felt nervous and that knowledge dissolved the feeling of uneasiness.

At that point it became clear to me that *my* dreams contained my own personal symbolism and my spiders meant something completely different from the definitions I had read in books. So I continued interpreting my dreams with the pendulum, loving every minute of it. I am always amazed by what I find and this has taken me on a journey of self-discovery beyond my expectations. If you choose to interpret your dreams using the pendulum, I hope you will enjoy doing so as much as I do.

Introduction

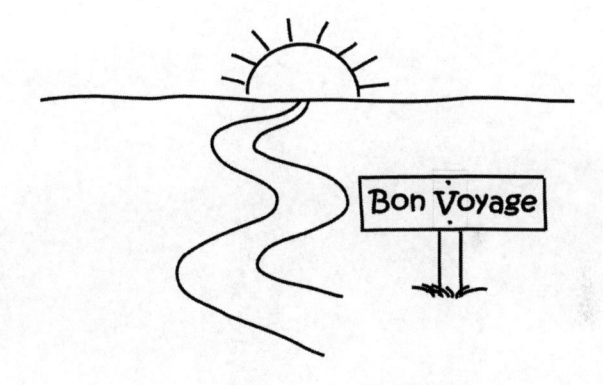

Three Important Points Before Going Further

- Only you can interpret your dreams
- The usefulness of your dreams will depend on your approach
- If someone doesn't remember their dreams, that's OK

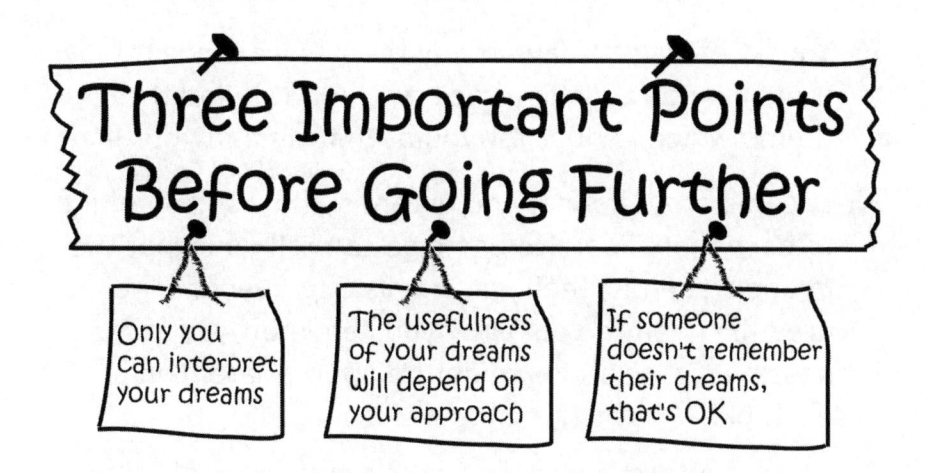

Only you can interpret your dreams

I have had people telling me: "I remember my dreams and I want to understand them. Could you use your pendulum and tell me what they mean?". And my answer was **NO**.

I want to make something very clear:

It is essential that *you* interpret *your* dreams.

This means **you** use the pendulum, **you** ask the questions and **you** find your own symbolism. Below are a few reasons why this is important.

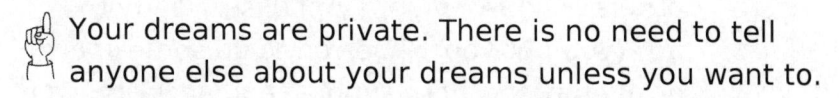

- Your dreams are private. There is no need to tell anyone else about your dreams unless you want to.
- You can go at your own speed. What you discover comes when you are ready to discover it.

How To Interpret Your Dreams Using A Pendulum

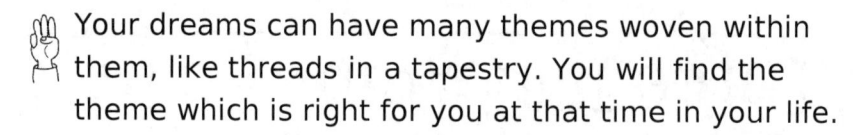

✌ Your dreams can have many themes woven within them, like threads in a tapestry. You will find the theme which is right for you at that time in your life.

✌ Dreams are personal and dream symbolism is unique to each individual. No one else can tell you what the images, sounds, feelings, smells and events in your dreams mean to you. Only you can know which possible associations might be appropriate. For example:

Words: we all have our own ideas about what a word means. For example, my husband was teaching a course on communication and asked 12 people to write down on a piece of paper what the word "success" meant to them. He ended up with 12 different answers which included "having a sports car" and "attaining Nirvana".

Objects: let's take shoes, for example. Someone dreams they are putting shoes on. "Shoes" could symbolise different things for different people. For some people "shoes" could symbolise being tight, confined or "boxed in" (depending on the shoes). For others "shoes" might symbolise "ready to go" (you put your shoes on to go somewhere) or even protection, support and security. For others "shoes" might symbolise fashion and elegance.

Three Important Points Before Going Further

People: as an example, we'll take the case when a person represents a quality. In one of my dreams my husband was with me. In this dream he symbolised discipline. No one else could have known that my husband possesses this quality unless they knew him well.

Animals: as an example, we'll choose a fish. Depending on the fish, it could represent a quality: flexibility, loner, sociable, etc... or a concept: beauty, happiness (after all, French people say: "heureux comme un poisson dans l'eau"). The possible associations are endless.

> **IMPORTANT**
> You need to **explore your associations** for words, objects, people, numbers, colours, sounds, smells, feelings that appear in your dreams. At first it takes time to find your symbolism and understand your dreams but with practice it becomes easier and quicker. (Trust me!)

> **EXTRA IMPORTANT**
> We all have different life experiences so our dream symbolism will be unique. It is for this reason that we are best suited to interpret our own dreams.

The usefulness of your dreams will depend upon your approach

If you approach your dreams with the attitude of "I am not good enough so my dreams certainly reveal my faults", then you will influence the whole process of dream interpretation and end up with information which will just confirm what you are already telling yourself during the day. In this case it is not worth spending time interpreting your dreams.

Three Important Points Before Going Further

But if:

- ✓ **you interpret your dreams because you are interested, not because you "should", "must", "ought to"; and**
- ✓ **you explore your dreams with a sense of curiosity and playfulness;**

then you will deepen your understanding of yourself and your life in a positive way.

If someone doesn't remember their dreams, that's OK

Although we all dream, not everyone remembers their dreams when they wake up. I have heard people say, "I don't remember my dreams. I *should* remember them. I *must* do something about it."

NO!

No one has to remember their dreams, and nothing has to be done about it.

Let things happen naturally.

A friend of mine said that her husband thought he never dreamed because he never remembered anything. But one day he got up and was very surprised because two dreams were very clear in his mind. He didn't do anything to make this happen, it just happened naturally.

How To Interpret Your Dreams Using A Pendulum

So What Are Dreams Anyway?

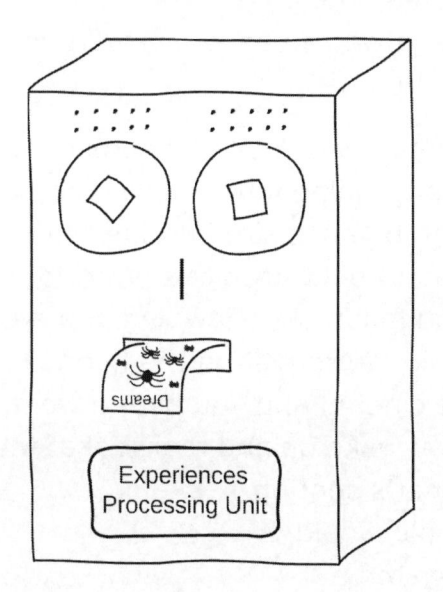

Experiences Processing Unit

> **NOTE**
> This book contains my ideas which are based upon personal experience. I don't claim any scientific or psychological expertise in this subject. I am sharing these ideas with you simply because I have found them useful. When you start interpreting your dreams using a pendulum you will make your own discoveries.

How To Interpret Your Dreams Using A Pendulum

It seems to me that dreams are the unconscious processing of our experiences. During the distractions of daily activities (family, work, watching TV, etc.) it is difficult to be aware of what's going on within ourselves, but when we sleep the busy-ness of our conscious mind calms down, and we can become aware of our inner processes via dreams.

Although dreams reveal our inner processing, not all dreams are worth going into deeply. For example, a noise like an ambulance siren during the night may make you dream about hospitals or accidents. Or you dream that you fall in the snow and you are cold. You wake up finding your duvet on the floor. Or you dream you are at the cinema and you hear a weird noise behind you. You wake up and realise that the noise is in fact your partner's snoring.

Another example would be when you watch a scary movie like *Jaws* and then you dream of a shark chasing you. These dreams are examples which we intuitively recognise as being obvious and not worth interpreting further.

14

So What Are Dreams Anyway?

But there are dreams which are striking, intriguing or worrying, and these are the ones that are interesting to interpret.

The information in dreams usually bubbles up in a metaphorical way. Much of the time people, animals, objects/things, numbers, colours, places, sounds, actions/events represent or symbolise someone or something else. So, to understand your dreams you need to understand *your* symbolism. It sounds like work especially because nobody else can tell you what your symbols represent. But, in fact, it is fun because it's like a puzzle. You find one symbol, then another one and so on and then the picture becomes clear. This is when you say: "Wow - this is what this dream means!"

It does happen that some dreams are very straight-forward. The best dream to illustrate this was one of my husband's. For a few months he was having red, scratchy eyes which didn't clear up. One night he had a dream where someone grabbed him by the lapels of his jacket, shook him and said "You are allergic to nuts!". It was extremely helpful and when he stopped eating nuts his eyes cleared up. This was a very easy dream to understand. Unfortunately only a few dreams are that blunt!

Symbols

* They depend upon an individual's culture and life experience – so a symbol doesn't have one meaning for everyone. It is for this reason that I don't use dream dictionaries.

* Symbols are simply symbols. There are no "bad" symbols or "good" symbols. Spiders could mean a good worker, speed, a trap or anything else, depending upon the person. There could be as many meanings for spiders are there are people in the world. Symbols like sharks, spiders, snakes, death, etc., don't necessarily represent something bad or unpleasant. In my earlier example spiders represented children because for me both behaved unpredictably. There was nothing "bad" about spiders or the unpredictability of children, simply a discovery of a similarity in behaviour.

> **IMPORTANT**
> The meaning of a symbol can change from dream to dream or it can be the same for a while. For example, sharks in my dreams represented doubts for a period of a year. Later sharks represented cleansing (after all they are the scavengers of the oceans).

So What Are Dreams Anyway?

Don't panic!

Even if it sounds like a challenge to understand your dream symbolism, it is not difficult. It is actually quite straightforward, enjoyable and rewarding. With practice you will have more and more intuition and you'll find short-cuts which will help you find the meaning of the symbols quicker.

How To Interpret Your Dreams Using A Pendulum

After interpreting your dreams for a while you will realise that there are several varieties of dreams. To understand the difference we can take the analogy of a conversation. It could be:

☞ different conversations on different subjects. You have a dream once on a subject and that's it.

☞ the same conversation on one subject repeated over and over again because someone hasn't understood. This corresponds to the same **recurring dream** with the same information repeating itself until understood.

☞ conversations on the same subject. These conversations sound different because different words are used but the topic is the same. This corresponds to dreams which superficially appear different but actually convey the same meaning. These are **reminder dreams**. I have had a lot of these dreams! This happened when I wrote down a dream, interpreted it and then let go of the information. For example, I had a dream whose meaning was "ground yourself". But I did not ground myself. A few weeks later I had another dream and its meaning was "ground yourself". Oops! I had forgotten about that!

☞ different conversations on a subject which is evolving. Each conversation would cover the latest development(s) of the situation or person. These

So What Are Dreams Anyway?

correspond to what I call **development dreams** and can occur later the same night or on another night.

☞ one conversation covering several topics. In this case the different parts of the same dream would involve different topics. In a conversation it is, normally, easy to realise when we have changed topics because we use sentences like "Now, talking about something completely different....", or "Let's move on to the next item on our agenda". Unfortunately dreams are not that explicit. What can give a clue that parts of a dream are on different topics is that the dream seems to jump from one thing to another. For example, you are in a house and begin to clean it. Then you jump to being in the street looking at shop windows. It is still the same dream but there is no continuity between scenes.

In all these dreams you discover advice, friendly warnings, progress reports, internal changes, etc. Your dreams are giving you feedback on what's going on within you.

From my experience of interpreting dreams over ten years, I have always found that the feedback is helpful and comes in a positive way. The understandings I have received from my dreams are like those that I get from a dear friend.

How To Interpret Your Dreams

As soon as possible after you wake up, write down **everything** you remember from your dream and the date. You can write the whole dream or simply use bullet points if you remember only fragments of the dream. If you remember only an image or a feeling then make a note of that.

When you have time, you can start interpreting your dream.

Reminder: The basics of using a pendulum are reviewed in the last chapter.

How To Interpret Your Dreams Using A Pendulum

First Thing to Find Out When Interpreting Your Dream

As mentioned earlier not all dreams require interpretation. To find out if your dream needs to be interpreted, read it, for example saying: "During the night of ..... (or last night) I dreamt that ..... (read your dream), and ask:

"Is this dream meaningful/significant/ important* for me?"

(* Choose whichever term you prefer.)

If the pendulum swings *Yes*, then continue with the questions in the next section (What To Do Next?).

If it swings *No*, then ask:

"Is this dream simply a processing-dream?"

What I call "processing-dreams" are dreams provoked by a movie you saw, a noise heard during the night (sirens, snoring ...), etc.

If it swings *Yes,* then let go of this dream and move on to another dream.

If it swings *No*, then ask:

"*Are there any* **scenes** *from this dream that are significant for me?*"

If it swings *Yes*, then go through the dream piece by piece, finding the scene or scenes that are significant. For example, imagine you dreamed that you had left a party and you were running in the street feeling rushed. You arrived at your house and couldn't find the keys to get in. You could ask:

"*Is the scene where I left a party significant?*"

"*Is the scene where I was running in the street feeling rushed significant?*"

"*Is the scene where I arrived at my house significant?*"

"*Is the scene where I couldn't find my keys significant?*"

If it swings *Yes* to one or more of these questions, interpret the scenes which are significant.

If it swings *No* to the question "*Are there any* **scenes** *from this dream that are significant for me?*" then perhaps it is the overall feeling of the dream that is significant. You could ask:

"*Is it only feeling rushed which is significant for me?*"

How To Interpret Your Dreams Using A Pendulum

If it swings *Yes*, then it is this feeling that needs to be explored.

Sometimes all you remember from a dream is a single image. For example, you wake up and the only thing you remember, is seeing a waterfall. You could ask:

"Is the image of the waterfall significant for me?"

You could also check sounds, numbers, smells, since one of these might be significant.

Now you know if the dream needs interpreting and if it is the whole dream, a scene from the dream, a feeling, an emotion, a single image, a sound, a number, a smell, ... that is significant.

If you have *No* answers to all these questions, then maybe now is not the right time for interpreting your dreams. Check if it's better to interpret your dream another time.

What To Do Next?

There are several ways to begin interpreting a dream. For example you could begin with:

☞ finding out what the dream is related to: family, work, an activity, ... ;

How to Interpret Your Dreams

👉 asking about anything that you find particularly striking; or

👉 going through the dream sequentially.

Choose the way that suits you best. These are guidelines to the approach and not a rigid recipe. You may start interpreting your dream sequentially, and then drift into what it is related to, or vice versa. This is fine.

Imagine that you have collected the following four dreams. Let's take your first dream.

Dream 1

"I was in a field which was covered with yellow flowers and there were lots of rabbits. They were eating the flowers. I was running after them but felt slow on my feet. Then I saw a group of people in the right-hand corner of the field. I also heard someone calling me from the left-hand corner of the field."

How To Interpret Your Dreams Using A Pendulum

You ask the initial question "*Is this dream significant for me?*" and the pendulum swings *Yes.*

If you work through this dream sequentially the first item is "I". In your dream what does the "I" represent? If you thought the "I" can be only one thing then you are in for a surprise!

Questions you could ask about the "**I**" would be:

"*Is the 'I' in this dream representing my whole being?*"

"*Is the 'I' in this dream representing a part of myself?*"

"*Is the 'I' in this dream representing an aspect of myself?*"

"*Is the 'I' in this dream representing my natural self?*"

"*Is the 'I' representing a position/role I am in?*"

When you are asking what a symbol represents, I think that repetition in the questions is useful because this aids your concentration and ensures that your questions are clear and precise.

Have a look at the glossary, page *xi*, to understand what I mean by whole being, parts, aspects and natural self.

If it swings *Yes for*:

- the "I" representing the whole being or the natural self then make a note of it and move on to the next symbol.

- the "I" representing a part of yourself then find out which part it represents such as your feminine side, masculine side, ego, etc.

- the "I" representing an aspect of yourself then find out if it is your emotional, mental, physical, energetic aspect. Always check if it is only one aspect that is represented. It can happen that the "I" represents two or three aspects simultaneously.

- the "I" representing either your position (*e.g.* nurse, director of company, teacher) or your role (*e.g.* father, mother, friend), then find out which one.

The information about who the "I" represents is the first piece of the puzzle so write it down and go on to the next symbol.

Check if someone or something is significant before trying to find out who or what they represent, this will save time.

The field:

"*In this dream is the field significant?*"

How To Interpret Your Dreams Using A Pendulum

If it swings *No*, then pass to the next item or person in your dream, which for this dream would be the flowers.

If it swings *Yes*, then ask questions to explore what the field represents.

"*In this dream is the field representing ...?*"

Could the field be life in general or your life in particular, your body, your work, the countryside, an open space, freedom, property, etc?

The yellow flowers:

"*In this dream are the flowers significant?*"
"*In this dream is the colour yellow significant?*"

Depending on the answers you can ask:

"*In this dream are the flowers representing ...?*"
"*In this dream is yellow representing ...?*"

The flowers and/or the colour could represent anything. For example, a quality (*e.g.* fragile, bright, colourful, ...), a concept (*e.g.* beauty, creativity, ...), an experience (*e.g.* sight or smell), an emotional response (*e.g.* happiness, cheerfulness), an activity (*e.g.* gardening), ...

How to Interpret Your Dreams

> The meaning of colours changes from person to person and culture to culture. So colours will represent different things to different people.

The rabbits:

"*In this dream are the rabbits significant?*"

"*Are the rabbits representing ...?*"

What could rabbits represent for you in this dream? What are **your** associations? For example, for one person rabbits could symbolise softness or gentleness or vulnerability. For someone else they could symbolise magic or healing. They could also represent activities, projects, distractions, opportunities, etc. You might want to check if the quantity of rabbits is also significant.

The rabbits eating the flowers:

"*In this dream is it significant that the flowers are being eaten?*"

"*Does it means ...?*"

Running after the rabbits but feeling slow on my feet:

"*In this dream is running after the rabbits significant?*"

"*Does it mean ...?*"

"*In this dream is feeling slow significant?*"

29

"Does feeling slow on my feet represent ...?"

What does feeling slow on your feet mean to you. Could it mean being stuck, out of control, tired, clumsy, grounded, held back, deliberate, ... Explore this feeling without forcing a meaning onto it or labelling it bad or good. Be curious!

If you can't find an answer now, let it go until another time.

The group of people:

"In this dream is the group significant?"

"Are the members of the group significant?"

"Does the group represent ...?"

"Is the number of people in the group significant?"

"Does the number mean ...?

"In this dream is it significant that the group is in a corner of the field?"

"Is it significant that the group is in the right-hand corner of the field?"

"Does the right-hand corner of the field represent ...?

Depending upon what the field represents, the left-hand or right-hand corners may be significant.

The person calling me:

"Is the person calling me significant?"

If it swings *Yes*, then the person may represent an aspect or a part of you, someone you know, a quality, ...

"Is this person representing my whole being?"
"Is this person representing a part of myself?"
"Is this person representing an aspect of myself?"
"Is this person representing my natural self?"
"Is this person representing someone I know?"
"Is this person representing a quality?
"Is this person representing someone in general terms?"

Let's imagine that Paul, who you know, is the person calling and in this dream he is representing a quality. What are his qualities? Do you think of him as being creative or impatient or a workaholic. You picked Paul because it is one of his qualities that you wanted to symbolise.

Alternatively, you may not need to know specifically who the person is, but simply who or what they represent in general terms.

How To Interpret Your Dreams Using A Pendulum

Once you know what the person represents then you choose the direction of the questions that follow accordingly. If necessary you might ask questions concerning action or location. For example:

"*Is the action of calling significant?*"

"*Is the location in a corner of the field significant?*"

"*Is it significant that the person is in the left-hand corner of the field?*"

"*Does being in the corner represent ...?*"

After you have found what the symbols represent you "weave" the meaning for your dream. The meaning comes out of the collection of representations. When you think you have understood what the dream means, ask:

"*Does the dream mean that ...?*"

"*Have I completely understood this dream?*"

If it swings *Yes* to these questions then you can take a break or go to your next dream.

It may happen that the pendulum swings *No* which means there is still something remaining to interpret. You could check if the *No* is because of the symbolism or because of the time-scale.

How to Interpret Your Dreams

You could ask:

> *"Have I completely understood the meanings of the symbols in this dream?"*

If it swings *No* then go through the symbols again and ask, for example:

> *"Have I completely understood the meaning of the field?"*
>
> *"Have I completely understood the meaning of the yellow flowers?"*
>
> *Etc.*

Whenever you have a *No* then explore that symbol further.

If it swings *Yes* to *"Have I completely understood the meanings of the symbols in this dream?"* then ask:

> *"Does this dream represent the past?"*
>
> *"Does this dream represent the present?"*
>
> *"Does this dream represent the future?"*

It may be that you were phrasing the meaning of your dream in the past tense but in fact the present or the future was the correct tense for that dream. This will become clearer in some of the following examples where two alternative time-frames illustrate how the interpretation would be affected.

33

Below are three versions among hundreds of possible interpretations. These are intended only to show how to take the collection of symbols and weave them together to form a pattern of meaning. The "I" was kept the same for these examples to show that, even with the same "I" there are several ways of interpreting this dream depending upon what the other symbols represent.

Version A

"I" = role as a manager of project
Field = project
Flowers = looks good
Yellow = not significant
Rabbits = parts of the project
Eating the flowers = situation looking worse
Running after the rabbits = getting out of control
Slow = can't cope
Group = co-workers
Standing in a corner = preoccupied with one part of the project, ignoring the rest
Person = someone preoccupied with another part of the project and attempting to bring the "I" to that part

Time = Present/Future
Meaning:
The project looks good at the moment but your co-workers are preoccupied and small things are starting to get out of control. If this trend continues the project may

not look good much longer. (This dream expresses concerns from deeper inside yourself.)

Version B

"I" = role as a manager of project
Field = large open area, room to move
Yellow Flowers = creativity
Rabbits = small distractions
Eating the flowers = taking away the creativity available
Slow = feeling stuck
Group = co-workers with limited "vision", only interested in one way of doing things
Person = another distraction

Time = Present
Meaning:
In your role as manager of a project you have more scope for being creative than you appreciate but you are wasting this opportunity by focusing on trivial distractions. You feel stuck because you aren't using the degree of creative freedom you have. Your co-workers are not thinking creatively and have restricted themselves to one corner.

How To Interpret Your Dreams Using A Pendulum

Version C

"I" = role as a manager of project
Field = your life
Flowers = life is looking bright and cheerful to you
Yellow = brightness
Rabbits = various activities
Eating the flowers = eating into time
Slow = low in stamina
Group = family
Standing in a corner = occupy only a small part of your life and attention, isolated
Person = someone who needs your help

Time = Past/Present	Time = Present/Future
Meaning: Your role as a manager of a project and your various activities have been consuming your time. This has caused you to isolate your family and also ignore someone who needs your help. This situation still exists.	**Meaning:** Your role as a manager of a project and your various activities are consuming your time. If you aren't careful then this will cause the isolation of your family and someone that needs your help.

Different people with different life experiences will have different interpretations.

Dream 2

"I was walking with someone in a large outdoor parking lot. There were only my old grey car and an helicopter there. For some reason, I knew that I could choose either one. The person with me said "It's good to take the helicopter". I said "I don't know how to fly it and I am afraid". The person said "Don't be afraid it will be ok". But I went to my old car and got in the driver seat. The person got in the back seat and we drove away."

Begin by checking if the dream or any part of it needs to be interpreted.

As before, let's imagine the whole dream is significant. So you can start with **discovering to what the dream is related**.

"*Is this dream related to my life in particular?*"
"*Is this dream related to work?*"
"*Is this dream related to family?*"
"*Is this dream related to relationships?*"

"*Is this dream related to life in general?*"

"*Is this dream related to my mental state?*"

"*Is this dream related to my emotional state?*", Etc.

– The mental state could be beliefs, thoughts, ...
– The emotional state could be feelings, mood, attitude, ...
– The physical state could be activity, health, ...
– The energetic state could be energy level, vitality, ...

Once you have found what the dream is related to, this will give you some ideas of which questions to ask when you explore the dream. Let's ask about the parking lot.

The parking lot:

"*In this dream is the parking lot significant?*"

"*Does the parking lot represent ...?*"

"I":

"*Is the 'I' in this dream representing my whole being?*"

"*Is the 'I' in this dream representing a part of myself?*"

"*Is the 'I' in this dream representing an aspect of myself?*"

How to Interpret Your Dreams

"*Is the 'I' in this dream representing my natural self?*"

"*Is the 'I' representing a position/role I am in?*"

Someone:

"*Is the person in this dream significant?*"

"*Is this person representing my whole being?*"

"*Is this person representing a part of myself?*"

"*Is this person representing an aspect of myself?*"

"*Is this person representing my natural self?*"

"*Is this person representing someone I know?*"

"*Is this person representing a quality?*"

"*Do I need to know specifically who the person is?*"

My old grey car:

"*In this dream is my old car significant?*"

"*Is my old car representing ...?*"

"*Is the colour grey significant?*"

"*In this dream is grey representing ...?*"

The helicopter:

"*Is the helicopter significant?*"

"*Does the helicopter represent ...?*"

How To Interpret Your Dreams Using A Pendulum

I am afraid:

"In this dream is being afraid significant?"

"Is it only fear that is stopping me from taking the helicopter?"

"Is the fear because ...?"

I went to my old car and drove away:

"Is getting into my old car and driving away significant?"

"Does this action represent ...?"

"Is the fact that I am driving significant?"

"Does it mean ...?"

"Is the fact that the person is in the back seat significant?"

"Does it mean ...?"

Now that you have found the meanings of the symbols in this dream you can ask:

"Does this dream mean ...?"

"Have I completely understood this dream?"

If it swings *Yes* to these questions then write down the meaning of your dream.

If it swings *No* then, like for Dream 1, check if the *No* is because of the symbolism and/or the time-scale (see page 33).

How to Interpret Your Dreams

Let's look at two possible versions, among many, of what this dream could mean.

Version A

Dream related to a life-choice/change.

"I" = ego
Person = natural self
Parking lot = life in general
My old car = your life
Grey = bland, drab, predictable
Helicopter = a new direction/way of life

Already with the understanding of these symbols the interpretation is simple.

Time = Present
Meaning:
An opportunity to choose a new way of life is available. The natural self is ready for the change but the ego is afraid. The ego prefers the life it knows and the natural self takes a back-seat.

Time = Future
Meaning:
An opportunity to choose a new way of life will become available. The natural self will be ready for the change but the ego will be afraid. The ego will want to choose the habitual and predictable routine. The natural self will take a back-seat.

This dream is information bubbling up from within. It lets you know that as things stand at the moment your tendency is to choose the habitual and predictable. The second meaning above is not a prediction of what will or must happen. You are free to choose differently if you wish.

Version B

Dream related to accomplishing some personal goal. For example learning a language.

"I" = ego
Person = natural self
Parking lot = life in general
My old car = old approach to learning (night classes near where you live)
Helicopter = completely different approach (like flying to the country and living there for a while)

Again the interpretation is straightforward.

Time = Present
Meaning:
You have the possibility to take a new approach to learning a language. The natural self is attracted to the new approach whereas your ego is afraid of it.

Dream 3

"I was in a two-storey house. I went upstairs and there was a room full of old furniture that was cluttering it. There was no place to move around. Then I went downstairs and it was a little run down and not very comfortable. I went back upstairs and started clearing up stuff."

First you find out if this dream is significant and if it needs to be interpreted. Working through sequentially you start finding out who the **"I"** represents.

Then move on to the house.

The two-storey house:

"Is the two-storey house in this dream significant?"

"Does the two-storey house represent ...?"

Depending upon what the house represents you could ask:

"Does the upstairs of the house represent ...?"

"Does the downstairs of the house represent ...?"

For example, the house could be your body and the upstairs your head. Or the house could be work, with the upstairs being management and downstairs a department.

The old furniture:

"Is the old furniture significant?"

"Does the old furniture represent ...?"

Depending upon what upstairs represents, the furniture might symbolise ideas, beliefs, habits, possessions, thoughts, ...

Clutter upstairs:

"Is this significant?"

"Does this represent ...?"

No place to move:

"Is this significant?"

"Does this represent ...?"

A little run down and not very comfortable:

"*Is this significant?*"
"*Does this represent ...?*"

Clearing up stuff:

"*Is this significant?*"
"*Does this represent ...?*"

Depending upon what the symbols represent, you may want to check if the action of going upstairs-downstairs-upstairs is significant.

Now that you have found the meanings of the symbols in this dream you can check if you have completely understood your dream. If not, then re-check the symbols and time-scale.

Let's look at two possible versions, among many, of what this dream could mean.

Version A

"**I**" = whole being
Two-storey house = your body
Room upstairs = head/mind
Room downstairs = the rest of the body
Old furniture = old beliefs/thinking
Cluttering upstairs, no place to move = getting in the way

Run down and not comfortable = body in need of attention
Clearing up stuff = clearing out old beliefs

Time = Present
Meaning:
Old beliefs/thinking are cluttering up your mind and getting in the way of paying attention to your body. You weren't consciously aware of this but your whole being has begun the process of clearing out the old beliefs.

Version B

"I" = whole being
Two-storey house = the old family business you work in
Room upstairs = management
Room downstairs = the business
Old furniture = old ideas about how to run the business
Cluttering upstairs, no place to move = getting in the way
Run down and not comfortable = not going well
Clearing up stuff = clearing up some old ideas that management has

Time = Present/Future
Meaning:
The old family business is not going well. You have realised unconsciously that this is because the old ideas about running the business haven't kept up with recent

changes. You want to clear up these old ideas which interfere with the business and you have started to do so.

As a result of this understanding you could approach management with suggestions of how to adapt to recent changes.

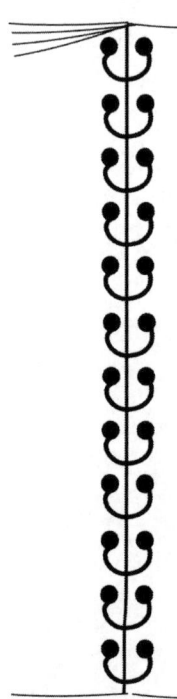

Dream 4

"I was in a house. I was alone in a ground floor room. The room was a bit run down. I decided to renovate it. I started by throwing away the furniture which was not comfortable. Then I painted the room with a nice colour which brightened the room. When it was finished I looked around and felt more and more comfortable."

First you find out if this dream is significant.

This dream might remind you of your earlier dream (3) so you could ask if it is a development dream or a reminder.

"Is this dream connected with the dream about ..... I had .....?"

"Is this dream a development from ...?"

"Is this dream also concerning ...?"

If it swings *No* to any of these questions then you can confirm that this is something new:

"Is this dream something new?"

Then interpret it as usual.

If it swings *Yes* for being a development dream then you could ask:

"Is the 'I' still representing ...?"
"Is the ground floor room representing ...?"
"Does throwing away uncomfortable furniture mean ...?"

Let's look at three possible versions of what this dream could mean.

Version A

If this is a development dream.

"I" = whole being
House = your body
Furniture = beliefs/thoughts
Throwing them away = letting go of the beliefs/thoughts
Painted the room = taking care of your body
Nice colour, brighten the room = improving mood
Feeling more and more comfortable = feeling good

Time = Present
Meaning:
Now that you have cleared up old beliefs/thoughts (see

Dream 3, Version A) you have started giving your body the attention it needs and you are feeling better as a result.

Version B

If this is NOT a development dream.

"I" = energetic aspect
House = your home
Furniture = stuff in the house
Throwing them away = letting go of the stuff
Painted the room, nice colour, brighten the room = changes once stuff out of the way
Feeling more and more comfortable = feeling good

Time = Present/Future
Meaning:
This dream is bringing to your attention the need to have more space. By clearing up your home you will feel better energetically.

Version C

If this is NOT a development dream.

"I" = emotional aspect
House = your life in particular (relationships with people)
Furniture = old emotional attachments
Throwing them away = letting go of the old emotional attachments

Painted the room, nice colour, brighten the room = feeling better emotionally

Time = Present/Future
Meaning:
You are in the process of letting go of emotional attachments from the past and will feel better emotionally.

IMPORTANT
This is about exploring and understanding your dreams and their symbolism. It is not about right/wrong or good/bad. There is nothing negative about dreams. Explore what information comes and ask yourself "Does this help me understand myself better right now?" If you feel that it is not helpful, then you can let it go. When something is important it does come back eventually.

REMEMBER
This book is meant to give you an idea of what is possible when you interpret your dreams. Unfortunately, I can't write down every single question that could be asked. **Explore around questions and your symbolism.**

Some More Examples of Dream Interpretation

This chapter is optional. You can read the examples below or go straight to the next chapter.

> ### Dream 1
> *"I went to work. When I arrived in my office I started working and suddenly collapsed. Someone came in the office and I heard this person say 'your heart is missing'."*

You wake up suddenly. What a nightmare! You put your hands on your chest to check your heartbeat just in case! After a dream like that if you want to go to your doctor to have a checkup then by all means do so. It is important to do what you feel is right for you.

When you feel ready you can explore your dream. Let any anxiety be replaced by curiosity. Seldom is something in a dream what it appears to be on the surface. Remember we are dealing with metaphors and symbols.

Even with this kind of dream it is best to check if it needs to be interpreted. If you have a *Yes*, then you can start with what is most striking.

Suddenly collapse:
> *"Is the scene where I collapse significant?"*
>
> *"Does this represent ...?"*

On first impression, collapsing might seem worrying but it is actually giving you a useful insight about the way you feel deep inside. This could show fatigue, stress, a sudden realisation, something coming to an end, ... Explore!

Your heart is missing:
> *"Is the sentence 'your heart is missing' significant?"*
>
> *"Does this represent ...?"*

Like the saying that someone's heart is not in what they are doing, this could be a lack of belief or motivation, boredom, ...

You could then follow up with questions about what it is related to? (work, home or an activity you do), who is the "I"? Who is the person talking to you?

As you did for the other dreams you would ask if you understood the dream.

Below are two possible versions, among many, of what this dream might mean.

Some More Examples of Dream Interpretation

Version A

Dream related to work

"**I**" = ego
Work = work
Person = natural self
Collapse = sudden realisation
Heart is missing = your heart is not in your job

Time = Present
Meaning:
You have suddenly realised that your heart is not in your work.

Version B

Dream related to daily routine

"**I**" = emotional aspect
Work = repetitive daily routine (home and work)
Person = feminine side (here representing creativity)
Collapse = "bored to death"
Heart is missing = no enjoyment

Time = Present
Meaning:
Your daily routine bores you to death because it lacks creativity. It doesn't bring you any enjoyment.

55

> ## Dream 2
> "I am in a big cage. I can breathe but not very well. Then I look around and see that there is a key in one of the corners of the cage and I take it. I open the door of the cage and I immediately breathe better."

Find out if this dream is significant and who is the "**I**". Then go through the symbols.

The cage:
>"Is the cage significant?"
>
>"Does the cage represent ...?"

I can breathe but not very well:
>"Is the sentence 'I can breathe but not very well' significant?"
>
>"Does this represent ...?"

The key:
>"Is the key significant?"
>
>"Does the key represent ...?"

The corner of the cage:
>"Is the corner of the cage significant?"
>
>"Does the corner of the cage represent ...?"

I open the door:
>"Is the sentence 'I open the door' significant?"
>
>"Does this represent ...?"

Some More Examples of Dream Interpretation

I immediately breathe better:
> *"Is the sentence 'I immediately breather better' significant?"*
>
> *"Does this represent ...?"*

As usual, check if you understood the dream.

Below are two possible versions of what the dream could mean.

Version A

Development from Dream 1

"**I**" = emotional aspect
Cage = work
Breathe but not very well = find work emotionally restricting
Key = an opportunity
Corner of the cage = a part of your work
Open the door = a way to change the situation
Breathe better = emotionally easier

Time = Present/Future
Meaning:
You find your work emotionally restricting. At the unconscious level you have recognised an opportunity to change this situation so that work will be emotionally easier. You could explore further this opportunity for change.

Version B

This is NOT a development dream
It is related to a relationship

"I" = ego
Cage = a confining relationship you are in
Breathe but not very well = feeling trapped
Key = a possibility
Corner of the cage = within the relationship
Open the door = a change in the relationship
Breathe better = feeling better

Time = Present
Meaning:
You feel trapped in your relationship with .... There is a possibility within this relationship for a change so that you feel better.

You may feel unconsciously that there is a possibility to change your relationship for the better and your dream is bringing this information to your conscious mind. You can use the pendulum to find out more about this possibility.

Some More Examples of Dream Interpretation

Dream 3

"*I was walking in China Town. I looked at the Chinese characters above the shops and told myself that it would be good to learn more about them.*"

I mentioned earlier that seldom is something what it appears to be on the surface. But it does happen that, like the dream above, which was one of mine, the interpretation is straightforward.

My Interpretation

"**I**" = whole being
China Town = China Town
Looking at the Chinese characters = interested in the Chinese characters
It would be good to learn more about them = It would be good to learn more about them

Meaning:
It would be good to learn more about Chinese characters.

I had been learning Chinese for a few years and then I stopped. After I had this dream I enrolled in a Chinese class again and I haven't regretted it. I enjoy the class very much.

> # Dream 4 (fragments of a dream)
> - I was walking in a street
> - It was night-time and it was raining
> - I was barefoot
> - I was going somewhere and I didn't know where

Even if you don't have the whole dream you can still work with the fragments you have.

First you need to check which fragments are significant so you ask:
> "*Is the scene where I was walking in a street significant?*"
>
> "*Is the fact that it was night-time significant?*"
>
> "*Is the fact that it was raining significant?*"
>
> "*Is the scene where I was barefoot significant?*"
>
> "*Is the scene where I was going somewhere and I didn't know where significant?*"

Then you would ask:
> "*Are the fragments part of the same meaning?*"

If it turns out that some or all of the fragments are unrelated then you interpret them accordingly (separately or together).

Some More Examples of Dream Interpretation

For this example let's assume that the fragments are part of one meaning, so you would ask:

"I":

"*Is the 'I' in this dream representing my whole being?*"

"*Is the 'I' in this dream representing a part of myself?*"

"*Is the 'I' in this dream representing an aspect of myself?*"

"*Is the 'I' in this dream representing my natural self?*"

"*Is the 'I' representing a position or role I am in?*"

The street:

"*Does the street represent ...?*"

Depending on who is the "I" and what is the street, the action of **walking** may be significant or not.

"*Does walking in the street significant?*"

"*Does it represent ...?*"

Night-time:

"*Does night-time represent ...?*"

Raining:

"*Does raining represent ...?*"

It is important in dreams to check possible symbolism of the time of day and weather. For example day-time might represent your conscious mind and night-time

61

might represent your unconscious mind. Rain might represent sadness, gloomy mood or being cleansed or grounded.

Barefoot:
   "Does barefoot mean ...?"

Going somewhere and I didn't know where:
   "Does going somewhere and not knowing where mean ...?"

As you did for the other dreams you would ask if you understood the dream.

Below are two possible versions of what the dream might mean.

Version A

"I" = energetic aspect
Walking in a street = progressing somewhere
Night-time = deep
Raining = cleansing
Barefoot = grounding
Going somewhere and didn't know where = echoes the "walking in a street"

Time = Present
Meaning:
Deep cleansing and grounding in energetic terms is in progress. (This is like a Progress Report.)

Some More Examples of Dream Interpretation

Perhaps your recent activities have contributed to this? Change of diet? Exercise? Bodywork? ...

Version B

"I" = mental and emotional aspects
Walking in the street = going somewhere
Night-time = dark
Raining = gloomy
Barefoot = exposed/unprotected
Going somewhere and didn't know where = lost

Time = Present
Meaning:
You are feeling lost and vulnerable at the moment.

You may want to re-examine recent choices or activities. Or perhaps you have reached a point in your life or work where you feel lost and vulnerable. Explore! In a positive way you can find out why you feel that way and what you can do about it.

How To Interpret Your Dreams Using A Pendulum

> ## Dream 5
> "*I was on a beach. A boat began to appear beneath the water, then rose out of the water and approached the beach.*"

You would find out who is the **"I"** and then ask:

The beach:
    "Is the beach significant?"
    "Does the beach represent ...?"

The sea:
    "Is the sea significant?"
    "Does the water represent ...?"

The boat:
    "Is the boat significant?"
    "Does the boat represent ...?"
    "Is it significant that the boat appeared beneath the water?"
    "Does this mean ...?"

Rising out of the water:
    "Is this significant?"
    "Does rising out of the water mean ...?"

Approaching the beach:
    "Is this significant?"
    "Does approaching the beach mean ...?"

Some More Examples of Dream Interpretation

Below are two possible versions among many.

Version A

"I" = whole being
The beach = conscious
The sea = unconscious
The boat = a feeling
Rising out of the water and approaching the beach = rising out of the unconscious and becoming more noticeable

Time = Past/Present
Meaning:
A feeling you were aware of unconsciously is now surfacing in your conscious awareness.

Are you aware of a vague feeling that has become noticeable recently? You could explore further which feeling it is and why is it surfacing now.

Version B

"I" = mental aspect
The beach = your life in particular
The sea = your environment
The boat = opportunity on a mental level ⇒ learning something new
Rising out of the water and approaching the beach = becoming available

Time = Present
Meaning:
An opportunity for learning something new is appearing in your environment.

You could ask questions about this opportunity that has been recognised unconsciously.

> ### An Image
> "A big jar with bluish-greenish snakes in it."

An image might not seem very much to work with, but once you begin asking questions then it is surprising how much you can uncover.

As you would for dreams you would ask:

>"*Is this image of a jar with snakes in it significant?*"

If it is significant, then you could begin by asking either:

>"*Is the jar significant?*"
>
>"*Does it represent ...?*"
>
>"*Are the snakes significant?*"
>
>"*Do they represent ...?*"
>
>"*Is the colour significant?*"
>
>"*Does it represent ...?*"

Or

>"*Is this image of a jar with snakes in it related to ...?*"

Some More Examples of Dream Interpretation

The image could be related to an aspect of yourself or to your work, home or life. Knowing to what it is related might help you interpret the image.

You could stop when you know what the jar and the snakes represent or you could go further. Let's say your image meant you were going through a healing process. You might also be curious about what provoked this healing. Did you have bodywork not long ago? Did you meet a friend and have a really good laugh? Did you eat something healthy? Did the healing just happen? After all, the body is an amazing organism!

I had an image like this once where the jar, which was an amphora, represented my body and the snakes symbolised healing. The fact that they were bluish-greenish was significant because at that time, for me, these colours were associated with healing. The meaning was clear – I was going through an inner healing process.

An image can often have quite a few details. For example, imagine the image was of a waterfall. Was it a still image or was there movement? Was it a tall or short waterfall? Was the water trickling or flowing strongly? Could you see what was around the waterfall (forest, mountain, snow, sky, …)? Was the water clean or were there pieces of wood or rocks or dirt in it? You would go through the details to explore and develop the meaning of the image.

> ## A Feeling
> *"The feeling of being late for something."*

Imagine that instead of an image you remember only the above feeling when you wake up. It may reflect something obvious such as a deadline at work or someone's birthday or anniversary. Or the feeling might represent something more subtle that will require some exploration on your part.

You would ask:

> *"Is the feeling of being late for something significant?"*

And

> *"Is this feeling related to ...?"*

Once you know what this feeling is about you can choose the questions accordingly. If you can't find why you have this feeling, it's okay. Just wait for another dream that will develop what this feeling is about.

> The image or feeling is the first clue that takes you deeper in your questioning – just like a detective story.

Tips For Dream Interpretation

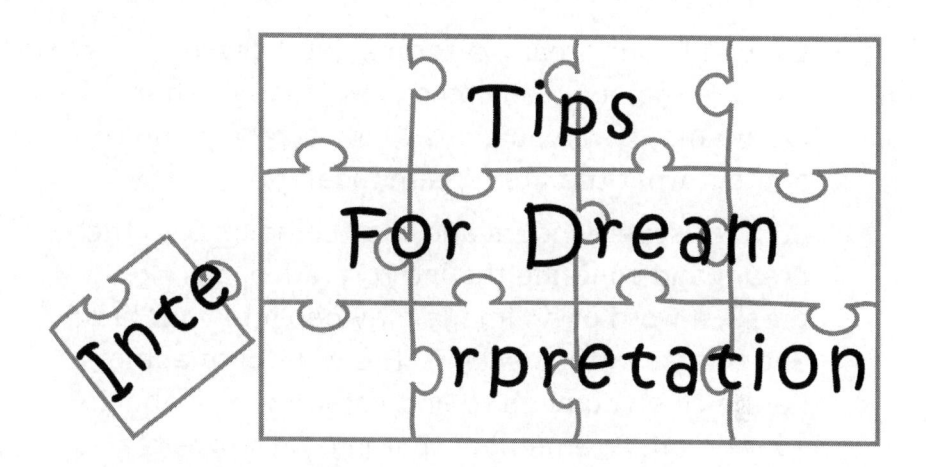

In the beginning, I would advise you to write down all your dreams so you develop your ability to recall them. Later, when you have more experience, you can check if a dream needs to be interpreted before writing it down. Keeping a dream diary will help you to understand your dreams better by revealing similarities and differences between them. Keep it in a safe and private place.

Interpret one dream at a time to avoid confusion.

Sometimes you may feel you don't know what questions to ask to find what a symbol means. That's okay. Don't let frustration take over. The ways to deal with this are:

☞ Let go of the symbol and try another one. For example, if you cannot find what a person represents then try finding out what the place, objects,... represent. These might give you a clue.

How To Interpret Your Dreams Using A Pendulum

☞ Let go of your dream, after making a few notes to indicate the point which you reached. Another dream may give you clues which can help you to find out what the first dream meant.

☞ Stop for several hours and then come back to the dream and continue the interpretation. During the break, a word or an image may pop into your head and this is worth checking. The word or image may be the clue you need to understand the symbol in your dream. I remember that in one of my dreams I had a sheepdog and I had difficulty finding out what it represented. So I stopped and did something else. What came to my mind suddenly was the image of the dog keeping the sheep together. "Keeping things together" was what, for me, the sheepdog meant in that dream and it fitted the overall meaning of my dream.

☞ Put the pendulum down and ask yourself "What are all the possible things ..... could represent for *me?*" See what associations come to your mind. Make a list of every possibility you can think of (including aliens from outer space if you want). Then pick up the pendulum to find which one(s) might be relevant. Ask questions even if they seem silly to you. There are no limits to what a symbol might mean or what questions could be asked. **Let your intuition and creativity guide you.** If nothing comes to mind then stop for a while.

Tips For Dream Interpretation

If your intuition of what an object means (for example, car = speed) fits with everything else in the dream then you can understand your dream easily. But sometimes, you may have a *Yes* that car = speed but this doesn't seem to fit with the rest of the dream very well. Explore around the word "speed". What else could be associated with that word or idea? Could it mean pace, doing things quickly, being rushed, out-of-control, ...?

Most of the time answers to related questions will be consistent. For example: You dream that three of your friends (Tina, Jackie and John) are talking to you. You have a *Yes* to the question "*Are the three people in my dream significant?*" and you have a *Yes* to each of the questions "*Is Tina significant?*"; "*Is Jackie significant?*"; "*Is John significant?*". It is clear that these people are significant and need to be taken into account when interpreting your dream.

However, sometimes your answers appear to be inconsistent. If you take the example above, you might have a *Yes* to the question "*Are the three people in my dream significant?*" and a *No* to the questions concerning Tina, Jackie and John individually. Although I found these inconsistencies frustrating when I started interpreting my dreams, I quickly realised that they were actually very interesting because they showed that I needed to consider more possibilities. So how can the three people be significant but not the three individuals?

What could be happening when you have inconsistent answers is:

☞ The answers *Yes* and *No* are letting you know that you are not quite there yet and you need to explore further. For example, you could ask "*Is it the number 3 that is significant?*", "*Is it the 3 people as a group that is significant?*", "*Is it significant that they are all colleagues from work?*", etc.

Depending on the dream, it could also be that:

☞ *Yes* and *No* means that it is not "this **or** that" but "this **and** that". For example, you ask the question "*Is this representing the mental aspect?*" No. "*Is it the emotional aspect?*" No. "*Is this representing the physical aspect?*" No. "*Is this representing the energetic aspect?*" No. Then you realise that it may involve 2, 3 or 4 aspects. So you would need to ask "Is this representing 2 aspects?" and then, depending on the answer, find which aspects are the ones you need to take into account. If you had received a *Yes* to your first question (mental aspect), you might have stopped there and not fully explored the remaining possibilities of what else might have also been included.

Never judge your dreams or yourself. Simply be curious about what comes from interpreting your dreams. **Dreams are neither right nor wrong, neither good nor bad.** The discovery of the meaning of your symbols needs to be done with an open mind.

Tips For Dream Interpretation

Beware of your assumptions "this *must* mean that...." or "this *couldn't* be relevant". Don't "force" dreams to fit what you think is happening in your life or what you want to happen. This is rationalisation. Ask and explore. With a positive attitude stay open to all possibilities.

If you have a dream that feels like a "warning" don't panic, it is simply advice. For example, imagine you interpret one of your dreams and the "warning" is that you are not grounded (you are more in your head than in your whole body). And being ungrounded means that you feel confused about what to do next in your life. So, the advice from the dream would be that if you ground yourself you would gain clarity.

It may happen that later you think of a question that you could have asked for one of your dreams but which you didn't think to ask at the time. This is okay. When you interpreted the dream you asked what was relevant at that point in time. This new question will become useful for later dreams. Or if you are really curious you can return to the dream and see what ideas are revealed by this new question. This is another advantage of keeping a dream diary.

If you get tired when interpreting your dream(s) it is best to take a break for a while and go back to it later when you feel rested. Interpreting your dreams is not a chore that must be finished by a certain time. Take your time and enjoy it.

How To Interpret Your Dreams Using A Pendulum

It doesn't matter if you don't remember your dreams all the time or if you decide you have enough for now and you want to take a break. This will let you integrate what you have discovered. You don't have to spend all your days interpreting your nights!

What about dreams that seem to be premonitions? I have never had premonitions so I cannot comment about them. However, the fact that I haven't had premonitory dreams doesn't mean they don't occur for others.

> **IMPORTANT**
> This approach is intended to be a **positive** way to interpret dreams, not something to become frustrated about. If you don't understand something this time, it will come back if it's important. Just enjoy finding out what you can at your own pace. And if something about a dream bothers you then you can talk to someone about it.

Basics of Using A Pendulum

Important Points

- When you begin practising dowsing, the way the pendulum swings for *Yes*, *No* and *Neutral* can be erratic or changeable. Check your swings for consistency each day before starting your questions. Once your swings have become consistent you don't need to check as often.

- In my opinion all pendulums are created equal. Crystal is no better than wood; wood is no better than metal, etc. Just look at the pendulums which are available and use the one that attracts you or

How To Interpret Your Dreams Using A Pendulum

that you *feel* like using. You can also create your own pendulum. It is important to go with your own feelings and not with what someone tells you.

- It doesn't matter which hand you use with the pendulum, as long as you are comfortable. My husband uses his left hand so that he can make notes with his right hand.

- Take time to integrate what you have learned. When you feel like you have had enough at any point in time, then pause, and take some time off from dowsing. Take as long as you need and go back to the pendulum when you feel ready to learn more.

- The pendulum is a tool to help you in your everyday life but it should not *become* your life.

REMEMBER
The magic is in you, not in the pendulum.

Tips

The Neutral Swing

Hold your pendulum and see if it begins to swing on its own. If it swings in a consistent way, this will be your *Neutral* swing. If it isn't swinging, then just hold your pendulum for a few minutes everyday until it swings. You don't need to do anything except wait patiently until the swing develops by itself. It is very important that the swings develops on its own without forcing it to happen. In my opinion it is good to have a swing for *Neutral* so that you can tell that the "engine is running" and you are ready to begin dowsing.

Make sure you come back to a clear *Neutral* swing after each answer so that you avoid confusing one answer with the next. The *Neutral* swing shows that you have finished with the answer to one question and are ready to ask a new question. This is essential for greater accuracy of your answers.

Yes and No

Once you have your *Neutral* swing then you *request* your *Yes* swing and you wait for it to show itself. After you have a *Yes* swing, then you *ask* for your *No* swing

How To Interpret Your Dreams Using A Pendulum

and you wait. You will end-up with three different swings which could be any one of:

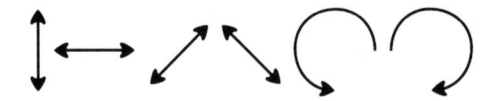

Remember to check your 3 swings each time you dowse until they are consistent and reliable.

Most of the time when you ask questions the answers are consistent. For example, you ask a question and you have a *Yes*. Then you ask a similar or related question for confirmation and you have another *Yes*. Great! That's easy! But it may happen that you have a *Yes* to the first question and a *No* to the second question. This is usually a sign that you need to explore more deeply.

When you frequently have *Yes/No* combinations, this may be because:

☞ You need more practice dowsing.

☞ The pendulum needs "cleansing" from other imprints, such as being handled by other people.

☞ It is the wrong time and/or place to use the pendulum (for example: you may be disturbed frequently by the phone; you need to leave in 5 minutes so you feel rushed; the room is quite noisy).

☞ Your questions are ambiguous.

Basics of Using A Pendulum

When you have only the *Neutral* swing even after a question, this may be because:

☞ You need more practice dowsing.
☞ You already know the answer or have already made your choice.
☞ It is too trivial to need a pendulum.
☞ You don't need to know the answer or it is not important at this time.
☞ It is the wrong time and/or place to use the pendulum.
☞ Your question is too vague.

Counting or Rating

This is helpful if you wish to estimate the amount of something, for example, how useful or beneficial something is. To count or rate something you can use a glass, your hand, the side of the table, anything that is convenient. You count how many times the pendulum bumps or taps the object and this gives you a number or a percentage. It might not tap at all which means it's zero! To avoid having large numbers you can use a scale of 0 to 10 taps for example where 10 taps = 100%.

Example

You would like to buy two things for your home (for this example I am assuming you are living alone). You know that both would be useful, but for now, you have just enough money to buy one. You can't make up your mind which one to buy.

You can ask "*How useful would it be for me to have .... now?*" and count with the pendulum. Then you ask the same question regarding the other object and compare the ratings for the two. You may have 70% (7 taps) for the first object and 20% (2 taps) for the second one. It is always best to go with your own feelings but if you are stuck and don't know which to buy then these percentages can help in making up your mind.

Example

You want to go to a course on painting but you are unsure if the course you have seen advertised in a brochure is the right one for you.

You could specify that 0 = unsuitable, 5 = satisfactory and 10 = excellent. You ask the question "*How good for me is the course on painting at (place), starting on (date) and taught by (name of teacher)?*". Keep in mind what you mean when you say "good". Is it the price? Is it the venue? Is it what they will teach? Then you count with the pendulum and see what the score is. If you have less than 5 taps, then you may want to find out

Basics of Using A Pendulum

more about the course before sending your money or you may want to look for other painting courses.

When You're Feeling Emotional...

A few years ago I was giving a *Dowsing Your Dreams* workshop and someone asked me about dowsing while feeling emotional. At that time I could not say very much about it because I had always avoided using the pendulum when I was emotional. Later I realised something important which has helped me greatly in learning about myself. I pass this on hoping that it will also help you. Here it is: *when you feel emotional, only ask questions about yourself and your feelings*. **Don't** ask about the person or situation to which you are reacting.

You may have already thought of this. Great! But for those who haven't tried it yet, here are a few suggestions for questions to ask (and to avoid) when emotional.

Example

Let's imagine you become angry whenever a colleague (Bob) speaks to you. You go home and still feel angry. So, when you have some privacy, you take your pendulum and ask questions.

✗ Don't ask "*Why is Bob driving me nuts at work?*" (Why questions can't be answered by *Yes* or *No* anyway.)

✗ Don't ask questions like "*Is he here to get me?*"; "*Is it all his fault?*"; "*Does he realise he is annoying me?*"; "*Is there a problem with the way he talks?*"

All of these questions focus on externals – Bob and the situation – and questions like these often seek to place the blame/responsibility elsewhere.

✓ Ask "*Is what I feel at the moment anger?*"
  ▸ If the answer is *Yes*, then explore what triggered your anger and why *you* are reacting that way. Is it linked to Bob? Or, you may be surprised because you may actually be angry at yourself. You can find out why!
  ▸ If the answer is *No*, then ask "*Is what I feel at the moment fear?*" If it is *No* to fear then continue asking questions to clarify *what* you really feel and then explore *why* you feel that way.

This is a very enlightening process because often we think we feel a certain emotion but after investigating we realise that the true emotion is a different one (*e.g.* behind anger could be fear and behind fear could be self-doubt). For example, you might be angry at someone because they always check your work. When you investigate you might realise that beneath the anger is fear that they will actually find a problem. And behind the fear you might realise that you have doubts about your ability to do your work. This self-doubt is the

Basics of Using A Pendulum

core emotion that is beneath the anger and fear. This is like "peeling an onion" layer by layer.

Let's go back to anger and assume it is simply anger that you feel and it is linked to Bob. Then find out what really makes you angry when he talks to you. For example, you may realise that his voice reminds you of someone you dislike! You can't ask Bob to change his voice because of this.

Example

You work in the same department as Lily. She has been working there for 25 years and you have difficulty understanding how she could stay so long in the same job especially because she says she is bored. Each time Lily comes into your office you feel uneasy. You don't understand why. So, when you have some privacy, you take your pendulum and ask questions.

- ✗ Don't ask questions like *"Should Lily get another job?"*; *"Is there something 'wrong' with her, like 'bad vibes'?"*; *"Is it because she doesn't like me?"*

- ✓ Ask *"Is what I feel at the moment uneasiness?"*.
  Find your feeling. Then ask *"Is Lily representing something (or someone) I'm reacting to?"*. The questions you ask will depend upon the answers you get. For example, you may find out that what makes you uneasy is that you know at some level that you are doing the same thing (staying although you are

83

bored) but you haven't admitted this to yourself and you don't like being reminded of this by Lily.

Example

When you go to the bank there is one cashier that you hope you won't have because you find him too slow. You are in the queue telling yourself "He is going to be busy with someone else, he is going to be busy with someone else, ..." and, of course, you hear the computer voice say "cashier number 6 is now free". You go there thinking "Here we go again!"

✗ Don't ask questions like "*Does he realise that he is driving me mad?*"; "*Does he need to change?*"; "*Is he doing it on purpose to annoy me?*", "*Is he going to work somewhere else soon?*"

✓ Ask questions like "*Do I like moving quickly?*" or "*Is it my temperament to be quick?*"; "*Am I an impatient person?*"; "*Do I like it when people move as quickly as I do?*" You may find out that you are an impatient person who has difficulty accepting people who are slower than you.

Example

Your neighbour (Mrs. Smith) is annoying you. She knows everyone in the block of flats where you live and chats with them in a friendly way. Although she is friendly with you too, you are annoyed by her.

Basics of Using A Pendulum

✗ Don't ask questions like "*Is Mrs. Smith chatting with everybody because she is bored at home?*"; "*Is Mrs. Smith really as nice as she seems?*"; "*Is she a gossip who wants to know what is going on around her?*"

✓ Ask "*Is what I feel at the moment annoyance?*"
- If it swings *Yes* to this question then continue by asking "*Is this annoyance related to Mrs. Smith?*". If it is a *Yes* then continue exploring the reason(s) for your feeling of annoyance.
- If it swings *No* to the question about annoyance then ask, "*Is what I feel at the moment jealousy?*". You may be in for a big surprise! It may swing to *Yes*. Are you simply feeling that way about Mrs. Smith because she succeeds in doing something that you would love to do but for some reason you don't? It may be that you don't have the time or you are shy or you feel you would not know what to say to people. Explore a bit more and stop when you feel it is enough for the moment. Learn about yourself gradually. Take the time to integrate what you have discovered.

I would like to say that the above example happened to me but in a different context. It was at work and one of my colleagues was going around the offices chatting with everybody. I was getting annoyed with her. For me, she was not working hard enough and she talked too much. I didn't even think of dowsing to understand the situation since I was convinced that it was all her fault if I was annoyed and she definitely needed to change. Finally, one day, I could not take this situation any longer and I dowsed to find out if it was time for me to find another job. The response was *No*. Then I asked "*Is it because she is chatty that I get annoyed?*" and I had a *No*. After a few questions concerning my colleague I realised I was getting nowhere. So I started to ask questions about myself, which eventually took me to the discovery that I was jealous of her. At work I wasn't chatty with people. I would try to talk to them but I didn't know what to say. I would go back to my desk and work. I would have loved to be like my colleague. I envied her ease in being able to go around and be chatty. The day I realised this, the situation at work changed completely. I didn't force myself to become more chatty, but I also didn't expect my colleague to stay in her office and work. This understanding was extremely helpful to me and certainly to the people around me since I became more relaxed at work.

The day I discovered this feeling within me I also discovered that I had been lying to myself. Before dowsing to understand the situation I kept telling myself that it was all her fault. I was okay and she wasn't. In hindsight, I realise that if I had paid more attention to what was going on within myself at the time, I would have felt the pangs of envy that were there from time to time. That day I learnt what it meant to be honest with myself and to accept that I have these feelings like everybody else. I have to say, it took me a while to digest this insight!

What you learn by asking questions is to know yourself, and by doing so you begin to "change" so that you are bothered less and less by certain people and situations. You can't change other people but it may be that as *you* change then the people around you will change too.

> **IMPORTANT**
>
> This process of questioning is **not** to find out whose fault it is (if in fact it is anyone's fault at all). It is to discover what is going on inside yourself so that a situation which makes you angry (or any other negative emotion) does not continue to affect you as it has. It is fascinating to see that when we understand what is going on within us, somehow the emotion seems to change, decrease or disappear completely.
>
> This process of discovery needs to be done with curiosity (What am I going to discover?) and open-mindedness (Whatever I discover will be okay for me because it is only a stepping stone.). There is no place for self-criticism and negativity in this process – only a desire to understand oneself better. This understanding then brings a better understanding of others.

Asking About Other People

If you asked about someone else, what would you do with the answers you get? For example: if you asked the question "Does my friend/neighbour have a physical/emotional/mental problem at the moment?" and if it swings *Yes*, what would you do then? Do you tell the person? Do you say nothing? Do you ask questions to know what is going on? Do you need to help? If so, how much would be appropriate without interfering? How do you know you are 100% correct? Even experts make incorrect diagnoses.

I think it is best to dowse about ourselves only and avoid asking questions about other people. As for friends or family, when they ask you to dowse for them I would recommend that you show them how to dowse so that they can do it for themselves. There is an old saying: "Give them a fish, they eat for a day. Teach them to fish and they eat for a lifetime."

Bits and Pieces

When you have an intuition that the time is not right for you to do something you probably already have an unconscious idea or plan. So you could dowse to explore more deeply and find out what it might be.

You can dowse to understand your own anxieties or worries. If these bouts of anxiety come during the night and keep you awake then it is helpful to get up and

Basics of Using A Pendulum

write down the feelings, the issues and the questions you would like to explore. Often just writing the questions down will be enough so that you can fall asleep when you go back to bed. Then, in the morning, you can dowse for answers to your questions.

Dowsing develops your intuition and can increase your sensitivity to energy, so I would recommend you learn to ground yourself well.

Sometimes I become very cold while dowsing or I get hungry. Some people have told me that they get warm. If you are cold, cover yourself well and drink something warm. If you are warm, open a window. Just go with what feels right to you and helps you stay comfortable.

It is also important to mention that when I started dowsing I realised that only 30-50% of my answers were correct. With practice the percentage increased significantly. The main reasons why the accuracy is often low at the beginning may be:

1. You doubt your ability, and your anxiety and tension interfere with the answers.
2. You are afraid of the possible answers.
3. The questions are phrased incorrectly. One example would be "Can I go see this person today?" The literal answer would certainly be *Yes* because you have the ability to see this person. That doesn't mean this person will be at home.

Another example would be "Is it a good idea to do this?" It may swing to *Yes* because it is a good idea in general but it may not be a good idea *for you* to do it *at this time*. With practice I realised how important it was to phrase the questions carefully. This resulted in much greater accuracy.

4. You go too quickly and you don't return to a definite *Neutral* swing in between each question.

Finally, below are a few things which I have found personally helpful. I mention these in case they might be helpful for you. Keep in mind that everyone is unique.

Vitamins and minerals: Depending on what I eat I take vitamins and minerals to supplement my diet. I realised that I needed to take more vitamins and minerals when I have been dowsing for longer periods.

Sugar: I often need a little bit of something sweet (a digestive biscuit or a square of chocolate) after a long dowsing session (20 minutes or more). If you feel that something sweet would be nice after a session but don't want to eat sweets then you may want to dowse for shorter periods of time. **CAUTION**: this is not an excuse to stop following any diet you are on, especially if it has been assigned to you for medical reasons. Avoid sugar and sweets if you are diabetic or have any other ailments where you must not have sugar.

Eating: I feel that I need to eat something before dowsing especially if the dowsing session is long. Maybe, in my case, it is to help me be more grounded.

A friend of mine said that she can't eat beforehand but she drinks a lot of water during and afterwards. For her water is very important.

Discover for yourself what is important for your comfort and health.

> REMEMBER
> Treat yourself gently,
> like you would treat a friend.

Now that you have read this book enjoy interpreting your dreams!